MOTHER HEN AND HER NEW BORN CHICKS

By Prince Albert King

A CHILDRENS ILLUSTRATED NOVEL

PRINCE A.KING
Author

Dedication:
TO MY GODSON JOHNATHAN KNOWLES
BY DR. PRINCE ALBERT KING,

PKDP HOUSE

P.O.BOX SB51712 - NASSAU N.P, BAHAMAS.

Author PRINCE ALBERT KING

ISBN: **9781070879246**

Printed in the
United States of
America.

ILLUSTRATED BY PKDP, INC.

Prince King Direct Printing House

P.O.BOX SB 51712, NASSAU N.P. BAHAMAS.

Mother hen has laid some eggs. There are five of them in her nest.

The baby chicks have beeped to each other so that they could hatch at the same time. Chicks have excellent hearing even inside the shell of the egg, First they make a crack in the shell. This is the very first stage in their birth. The crack gets bigger and bigger and bigger, until it goes all around the egg shell. The baby chicks use an egg tooth to break the shell. This tooth is located on the beak of the chick. Finally the baby chick, push and push until the shell pops completely open into two parts. This work takes all day long. Wow a whole new world is open to the chicks. Mother hen says "Welcome to the world my children"

The chicks says "chirp, chirp" which in chicken means "hello mommy"

Just hatched, the babies are wet and sleepy from all that hard work. Their eyes start to close down. like all new born babies they try to fight sleep, the countdown is on ten nine, eight, seven,

six, five, four, three,
two, one and they
are finally
overcome; eyes
closed, out cold.

In about twenty-four hours the chicks are dried off and know how to walk, see and hear mother hen clucking clearly. They still have a problem keeping their eyes open. They are all

very tired and
cuddles together.

the next day mother
hen takes her chicks
for a walk. The

chicks follow their mon around. Mother hen teaches them how to peach the ground to pick up worms, insects, grains and other food thrown to them by the farmer. Mother hen uses different clucking sounds for different reasons. The chicks understand her and can tell the difference between their mom and another hen.

In about eight days their wing feathers start to grow out. Later at fourteen days more feathers have grown out of different colors and sizes. Some are speckled, white, black or brown. Now it is time for the tail feathers to come out and grow. And the chicks will start to flap their wings to remove dirt and to keep their feathers clean. They learn to sense danger by avoiding other animals. At two months the chicks have red combs showing on the top of their heads and adult feathers are present. The chicks can do short flights flapping their wings. Don't you think that the chicks are so adorable?

Prince Albert King books written by this author of various genre, which can be ordered on amazon.com from this link:

https://www.amazon.com/-/e/B07KSLD5KG

Books by Prince Albert King

These are the books on Amazon's Prince Albert King page.

Adopted An adult novel by Prince A.King: Adopted (1)

Paperback
Current Sales Rank: #2,914,370 in Books
Average Review: There are no reviews yet

Spiritual Sickness By Prince Albert King, Th.D.: Gods will to heal me and you (1)

2 Editions
Current Sales Rank: #21,478,296 in Books
Average Review: There are no reviews yet

THE BAHAMIAN JOHNNY CAKE RUN (1)

2 Editions
Current Sales Rank: #6,298,899 in Books

The chickcharnee prince: A SERIES IN THE CHICKCHARNEY SAGA (1)

Paperback
Current Sales Rank: #347,898 in Books

Albert and the chickcharney birthday party: Bahamian chickcharney birthday party (3)

2 Editions
Current Sales Rank: #8,071,946 in Books
Average Review: There are no reviews yet

Adopted An adult novel by Prince A.King: Adopted (1)

2 Editions
Current Sales Rank: Unknown

The Bahamian Sea Prince (The sea King)

Paperback
Current Sales Rank: #21,480,107 in Books

THE BAHAMIAN SEA PRINCE : SECOND EDITION BOOK 1 (THE SEA KING 2)

Kindle Edition
Current Sales Rank: Unknown

The Bahamian Sea Prince (The sea King Book 2)

Kindle Edition
Current Sales Rank: Unknown

THE BAHAMIAN SEA PRINCE: SECOND EDITION BOOK 1 (THE SEA KING SERIES)

Paperback
Current Sales Rank: Unknown

The chickcharnee Forest: enchanted forest (chickcharney series saga Book 2)

Kindle Edition
Current Sales Rank: #3,293,485 in Kindle Store

The Chickcharney Enchanted Forest (chickcharney series saga)

Paperback
Current Sales Rank: #2,914,371 in Books

Books by Prince Albert King

These are the books on Amazon's Prince Albert King page. Click on any book below to view additional product details or submit corrections.

Page 2 of 2 (20 items)

Sort by

| Title: A to Z ▼ |

Chickcharney Halloween: Trick - O-Treat (Chickcharney saga series)

2 Editions
Current Sales Rank: #2,914,369 in Books
Average Review: There are no reviews yet

The chickcharney prince: The Chickcharnee Prince (1)

Kindle Edition
Current Sales Rank: Unknown

THE NIGHT BEFORE CHICKCHARNEY CHRISTMAS: CHICKCHARNEY SERIES SAGA BOOK 5 (CHICKCHARNEY SERIES BY PRINCE A. KING)

2 Editions
Current Sales Rank: #347,897 in Books

Deliverance from Bitterness: Spiritual Sickness book 3

2 Editions
Current Sales Rank: Unknown

NOTHING FOR CHRISTMAS BY PRINCE ALBERT KING,Th.D.

Kindle Edition
Current Sales Rank: Unknown

paperback Edition

SPIRITUAL SICKNESS 2 A Series fighting Panic Attacks: Fighting Panic Attacks

Paperback
Current Sales Rank: #347,895 in Books
Average Review: There are no reviews yet

SPIRITUAL SICKNESS book2 A Series fighting Panic Attacks: Fighting Panic Attacks

Kindle Edition
Current Sales Rank: Unknown
Average Review: There are no reviews yet

VIOLET TRAPPED IN THE CYCLE OF DOMESTIC ABUSE.

TRAPPED IN THE CYCLE OF DOMESTIC VIOLENCE

PRINCE KING

ADOPTED AN ADULT NOVEL BY PRINCE A.KING

Adopted

PRINCE ALBERT KING

PRINCE KING

The
chickcharnee
prince

The Chickcharnee
Prince

THE BAHAMIAN SEA PRINCE

SECOND EDITION BOOK 1

PRINCE KING

The Chickcharney EnchantedForest By Prince Albert King

PRINCE A. KING

THE LAST OGRE

A CHILDREN'S ILLUSTRATED FAIRY TALE

PRINCE KING

THE MYSTERIOUS SEA MONSTER BY OCTAVIA DEBORAH VICTORIA KING

Illustrator PrinceKing

Albert and the chickcharney birthday party

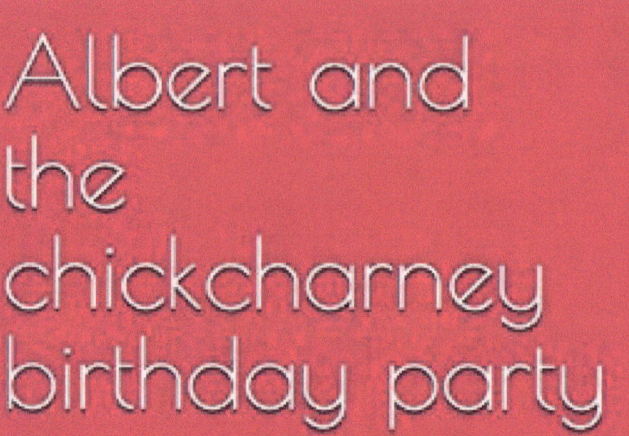

Bahamian chickcharney birthday party

Prince King

THE NIGHT BEFORE CHICKCHARNEY CHRISTMAS

CHICKCHARNEY SERIES SAGA BOOK 5

PRINCE KING

PRINCE KING

NOTHING FOR CHRISTMAS BY PRINCE ALBERT KING, Th.D.

THE
WITCH

A SERIES
PRINCE ALBERT KING

Violet a frictional illustrated Novel by author Prince A. King

Prince Allen King is a Bahamian author and illustrator of adult graphic literature and a visual provocateur. Additionally, Prince A. King a Bahamian business man and website designer.

violet

an adult illustrated novel of fiction

ZION'S BIRTHDAY PARTY

PRINCE KING

The Bahamian Sea Prince

Prince King

Spiritual Sickness By Prince Albert King, Th.D.

Gods will to heal me and you

Bishop Prince King

The Sea king A juvenile Teen and young adult fiction novel

The Sea king by prince king

Prince King

Chickcharney Halloween

Trick -O-Treat

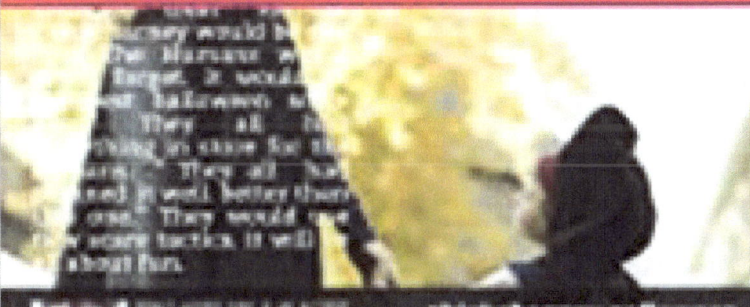

chickcharney halloween

Trick -O-Treat

BOOKS ARE AVAILABLE IN BOTH KINDLE
EDITION AND PAPERBACK

Chickcharney Halloween

Trick -O-Treat

PRINCE KING

prince king

Deliverance
from
Bitterness

Dr. Prince Albert King is a
Bahamian author who lives in
Nassau, New Providence,
Bahamas. He has written over
28 books of different genre,
which can be ordered on
amazon.com

www.ingramcontent.com/pod-product-compliance
Lightning Source LLC
Chambersburg PA
CBHW050824290526
45792CB00001B/249